Danbury and Little Baddow
in old picture postcards

by Peter Came

European Library ZALTBOMMEL / THE NETHERLANDS

GB ISBN 90 288 3492 3

© 1987 European Library – Zaltbommel/The Netherlands
Fourth edition, 1996: reprint of the original edition of 1987.

INTRODUCTION

Danbury and Little Baddow are adjacent parishes situated on a high well wooded ridge between Chelmsford and Maldon in central Essex. Topographically and historically both parishes share a good deal in common. Little Baddow occupies the northern part of the ridge and Danbury the southern but highest part. The name, Danbury, is derived from the stronghold of the Daeningas, a Saxon tribe that occupied the territory between Danbury and the sea. The name Baddow is probably derived from Beadewan, the old name of the Chelmer River which forms the northern boundary of the parish.

The settlement pattern within each parish at the turn of the nineteenth century was similar. Neither parish showed any inclination towards a grouped village. Danbury lay on an east-west highway and along this road from the Park to the church was 'The Street', a discontinuous straggle of houses. Eves Corner, Runsell Green, the northern part of the Common and Bicknacre showed some tendency to nucleation. Large areas of the parish contained isolated farms and cottages and even the manor house was isolated well to the west of the village. Little Baddow was similar. Its main spine ran north-south and along this road, descending northwards, was a discontinuous straggle of development. There was some nucleation around Coldham End and Wickhay Green, but elsewhere, like Danbury, isolated farms and cottages were the rule rather than the exception. Even the church and the hall were isolated a mile away from the village.

Both parishes show similar population patterns. Danbury was the larger settlement. In 1801 its population was 768 and Little Baddow's 456. Both parishes showed increases to 1861. Danbury had reached 1,113 and Little Baddow 605, but both declined after the agricultural depression of the 1870s and figures respectively for 1901 were 841 and 510. The 1881 census highlights some of the social effects. In Danbury 15 out of the 246 houses were unoccupied and in Little Baddow 10 out of 139 houses were in the same plight. Many large houses were occupied by bailiffs and some smaller farmhouses had been turned into tenements. Even so, the population was not immobile. Less than half of the population in each parish had actually been born there. Admittedly many had been born in adjoining villages but 14 per cent in Danbury and 8 per cent in Little Baddow had been born outside Essex. The Danbury statistic is high, but sometimes whole households, like that of the Bishop's at Danbury Palace moved, as self contained units, into the village.

In addition to the already established churches in both parishes, Little Baddow had a Congregational Church, but Danbury did not. Whether or not it was that Danbury was more sectarian, but between 1890 and 1925 a rash of chapels grew up: on Danbury Common, where there were two; at Gay Bowers, Copt Hill, Runsell Green and White Elm. Church of England schools were already established in both parishes and in addition there was a British School (closed 1895) at Little Baddow. A piped water supply was laid on to most parts of Danbury and Little Baddow respectively in 1892 and 1896.

Danbury and Little Baddow's proximity to Chelmsford and London, 35 miles away, had an impact on this area, for following the general depression of the mid-1880s, the area wore a prosperous ethos. Already guide books were extolling the virtues of this naturally beautiful area. Annie Berlyn (1894) wrote of the 'beautiful ferny, flower bedecked lanes that lead to Danbury Hill. On either side the hedges overflowing, according to season, with sweet hawthorn and trailing vines and bracken, dog roses, and honeysuckle and convolvuli, stretch across the path high overhead till almost meeting midway, they make veritable groves of these picturesque lanes, that lead, first to 'The Rodney' and further to the church...' at Danbury.

These ideas of a beautiful rural retreat were being taken up by those from urban areas and in turn the villages were responding. Not only were there quite substantial houses being built in the area for businessmen from Chelmsford and London from the mid-1890s onwards, but this was later aided by the Chelmsford-Danbury 'bus service' instituted in 1905. Local residents were also encouraging the tourist. The Rodney had been opened as a Pleasure Garden about 1885 and the Danbury Griffin was responding with stabling and garages for cars. First the bicycle, then the bus and ultimately the motor car were to help change the two parishes between 1900 and 1930. The low population figures for 1901 were dramatically transformed by 1931.

Danbury increased from 841 to 1807 and Little Baddow from 510 to 751.

Danbury's situation on a main road made it more vulnerable to exploitation with one petrol filling station and two purpose built garages, two cycle dealers, four cafés, about 15 shops as well as two housing estates laid out with their own roads before 1930. Not being on a main road, and lacking some of the more modern amenities, Little Baddow's development was more discreet and slower. There were only five shops, two public houses and no garage by 1930. Following the First World War many of the craftsmen such as the harness maker, wheelwright blacksmith and boot and shoe maker, gradually gave way to changing technology and access to national markets. But other industries such as building, winning gravel and bat making flourished as did poultry and apple farming. By 1930 it was already clear that both Danbury and Little Baddow were poised to become a dormitory area of the London commuter belt.

This volume is in no way meant to be a complete history covering the period between 1880 and 1930, but it is hoped that it will present some visual idea of the changes that took place in Danbury and Little Baddow between the two dates indicated.

My grateful thanks to the following for their help: Bakers of Danbury; the late Mr. H.W. Baker; Mrs. E. Barlow, Mr. H . Benham; Dr. R. Buick Knox (RBK); Mr. R. Came; the Chelmer & Blackwater Navigation Co.; the Essex Record Office (ERO); Chelmsford Central Library; Mr. and Mrs. J. Gibson, custodians of the Parish Chest (DC); the late Mrs. M. Hopkirk; Dr. A. Knightbridge; Mrs. F. Lucy, Mrs. B. Opie; Mrs. D. Potter; Mrs. K. Miller; Mr. C. Reynolds; Mr. and Mrs. E.W. Roast; Mrs. S.V. Rowley (SVR); the late Mrs. G. Royce; the late Mr. W. Wackrill; Mr. and Mrs. R. Warsop; and lastly to my wife Wendy, who has carried out all the typing.

This volume is dedicated to the memory of my parents, Frederick James Came (1903-1973) and Gladys Mary Came (1904-1985), both of whom lived in and shared my interest in this locality.

1. Danbury Church, c1905. The church, sited on the highest part of the Danbury-Little Baddow Ridge 365 feet above sea level, stands within an oval earthwork dating from about 500 BC. The earliest parts of the church date from the end of the twelfth century. This photograph shows the tower of about 1330 still covered with plaster; the spire rebuilt after the devil's visit in 1402; and the south aisle and south-east aisle respectively rebuilt and built at the restoration of 1866-1867. A foundation stone for the south-east aisle was laid by the Bishop of Rochester then residing at Danbury Palace. On the extreme right is the village water tank, erected in 1892. Water was pumped up to this point from Buell Well on Danbury Common and from this tank water was fed by gravity to most parts of the village. After 1893 water was conveyed to East Hanningfield, Rettendon and Woodham Ferrers. Yet another extension was made in 1896 to include Horne Row, Little Baddow, Battlesbridge, Runwell and parts of Sandon. The Rectory is shown on the left (see fig. 18).

ST. JOHN THE BAPTIST, DANBURY. 1785

Fred Spalding & Sons
Photo
Chelmsford
Copyright

2. Danbury Church, c1900. This shows well the arcade and north aisle of about 1300. The church is probably decorated for the Christmas festival. All the fittings shown are of nineteenth century date. The font was transported from London and installed in 1857. All the pews, apart from those to the left of the font in the nave, date from the restoration of the church by George Gilbert Scott in 1866-1867 which cost £3,780. Many of the 'poppy heads' of the north aisle pews were not carved until this century. A number are carved in the form of the regimental badges of soldiers stationed in the village in the First World War. The pew end nearest the north door was paid for by the Girl Guides. The pulpit, carved by John Matthews, and the choir stalls are all of 1866-1867. To the left of the pulpit is a slow combustion stove which was the church's only source of heat until Mr. and Mrs. Charles Parker of New Riffhams presented a new heating system in 1906. Redecoration of the north aisle followed in 1908.

3. Danbury Palace, c1900. This house, probably the third to exist in the park, was built in 1835. It was designed in a neo Tudor style by the architect, Thomas Hopper, and Mrs. Round. In 1845 the palace was purchased as a residence for the Bishop of Rochester whose new diocese spread north of the Thames to include Essex, Hertfortshire and Bedfordshire. The 96th Bishop of Rochester, George Murray, built on the chapel, left, before he retired in 1860. His successor, the 97th Bishop of Rochester Joseph Wigram, was here until 1867 to be replaced by the 98th Bishop, Thomas Claughton. Dr. Claughton became the first Bishop of St. Albans in 1877 when that part of his diocese that lay north of the Thames was formed into a new diocese. Dr. Claughton retired in 1890 but continued to live here until his death in 1892. He was buried at St. Albans Abbey. *He left the memory of a good man, kindly and moderate just the kind of man a diocese would like to remember as its first bishop* (Owen Chadwick).

DANBURY PARK. 1802

Fred Spalding
Photo.
Chelmsford.
Copyright

4. Danbury Park Lakes, c1900. The three existing lakes were formed when the park was laid out about 1290. This view shows the central and largest of the lakes, covering 2.1 acres, with its Gothic ornée boathouse. One of the early annual treats for the Danbury School children was 'young Mr. Murray' rowing them on this lake and 'the one that sang the best had the longest ride'. The owners of the park often opened it for parish events. Dr. Claughton entertained the parish to a 'capital supper' for the Golden Jubilee of 1887. At the 1902 Coronation 500 sat down to a dinner when the park and gardens 'were thrown open to all by the kindness of Mrs. C. Hoare'. Again in 1911 celebrations were held here for the Coronation of George V at the invitation of Lieutenant Colonel The Honourable Alwynne Greville, 'where all over 14 sat down to a dinner followed by sports'. General and Mrs. J.T. Wigan came to live at the Park in 1919 and they, too, allowed village functions, such as the Annual Flower Show, to take place here.

5. Main Road, Danbury, c1920, looking west. On the right near the telegraph pole is the Bell Inn, parts of which are sixteenth and eighteenth century in date. The name of the inn is probably associated with the legend of the Devil stealing the largest bell from Danbury Church and unable to carry it any further he dropped it in Bell Hill Wood. From the 1740s to the 1790s the Osborne family were landlords and in their time the local bell ringers quaffed ale here at the expense of the Landisdale Charity. Frederick Gladwell was another long serving landlord from about 1870 to 1897. From then on until 1930 there were a number of landlords including Henry French, Owen Pryce, Rosina Newcombe, Elijah Brice, Frances Fordham, E.G. Clinkscales and Mrs. Cheyne. The building to the Chelmsford side of the inn was probably once a stable and later a 'bus shelter'. Although the early steam 'buses reached the Griffin, the later petrol 'buses had to terminate at the Bell. The pair of villas, right, were built circa 1900.

DANBURY. 857

Fred Spalding
Photo
Chelmsford
Copyright

6. Bell Hill, Danbury, c1895. This hill was so called because there was a public house at the bottom of this hill from the eighteenth century onwards known as the Bell. In the distance is Danbury Park owned by Hugh Hoare, Esquire, who kept a dairy herd. To the left is the Blacksmith's that was kept by Richard Pickman in 1840 and much later by John Bush who was there from about 1899 to 1948. He was the last blacksmith in the village. The smith's shop, and his house, hidden from view, has the characteristic round headed windows of properties once owned by the Lord of the Manor. Berkeley Cottage, on the right, is of seventeenth century or earlier date. In 1840 it was owned by John Blatch, then described as one of the 'gentry', who must have been the father of John Blatch, junior, who was a surgeon in the village in 1863. Berkeley Cottage was part of the Riffhams' Estate and when it was sold in 1918 it was being rented by Mr. C.A. Ager at £15 a year.

7. Elm Green, Danbury, c1890. This triangular green had probably attained its shape before the sixteenth century. Elm Green is named on a map of 1758 and was known as 'Elms Green' in 1777. In 1893 there were 'three fine lofty elm trees having a public seat at their base, where the weary traveller may rest and enjoy the wide prospect of the rolling country, stretching from the German Ocean, across Essex into Hertfortshire'. These three elms had been planted to honour the Jubilee of King George III in 1810 and the seats were set up in 1887 to mark the Jubilee of Queen Victoria when three other elms were also planted. The 1810 trees became old and unsafe and had all fallen before the War Memorial was set up in 1920. This photograph shows well Danbury's rural aspect of those days with the Maldon road running left between the houses and cottages. One of the cottages to the right of the road was occupied in 1881 by Albert Hoar, builder.

8. War Memorial, Danbury. This memorial was set up on Elm Green on the site of one of the three large elms that were planted on the Green in 1810. The memorial was designed by Sir Reginald Blomfield RA, one of the principal architects to the Commonwealth War Graves Commission, and is made of Portland stone. This same design of cross is repeated in the many cemeteries between the Ypres salient and Dunkirk, but there are only a few crosses of this distinctive design in England. The memorial was unveiled by Field Marshal Sir William Robertson on 31 July 1920, in the presence of Brigadier General J.T. Wigan; Major General F.F. Johnson, Chairman of the Parish Council; Lieutenant Colonel G.W.T. Prowse, Chairman of the Memorial Committee; Mr. Justice Rowlatt; relatives of the fallen; service and ex-service officers and men; parishioners and friends. The Rector, the Reverend J.B. Plumptre, addressed these words after the unveiling: 'We dedicate this cross in thankfulness to Almighty God and in memory of the Men of Danbury who have died gloriously for their country.'

Riffhams Danbury

9. New Riffhams, Danbury, c1910, was described in 1848 as 'a handsome mansion with sylvan grounds on the north side of the parish'. This 'lodge' was built in 1817 by John Robert Spencer Phillips, Esquire (1787-1874), in fashionable white brick. A stream flowing from Bell Hill Wood was dammed to form a lake to add grandeur to the setting of the house. Mr. Spencer Phillips died in 1874 and the house was let, first, to Mrs. E. Kirk who presented the eagle lectern to Danbury Church in memory of Maurice Kirk who was killed in the Boer War in 1900; and, secondly, about 1904 to Mr. and Mrs. Charles Parker who allowed the Danbury Flower Show and Danbury cricket matches to be held there. Mr. Parker was a Magistrate and in 1905 churchwarden. He presented a new heating system to Danbury Church in 1906. About 1910 John Charles Spencer Phillips Esquire, a Magistrate, made Riffhams famous for its pedigree herd. In 1928 Sir Adam and Lady Ritchie were here followed by Sir Follett Holt, a railway engineer, about 1933.

10. Old Post Office, Danbury, c1900. George Spalding (1830-1923) set up a bakery business here in the 1840s and by 1870 he had added to this the job of village carrier. This latter function he gave up when he took over the Post Office about 1875 and its business was carried on in the right hand room of the main house. In the 1890s George's daughter, Margaret, was assisting in the Post Office and by then the room shown to the right had been added to cope with the increased business. Meanwhile George had given up his bakery business and in 1909 he retired to Corner Cottage. Before George retired another daughter, Mrs. Clara Langman, had been appointed sub-postmistress. As business continued to increase so the small room had to be rebuilt about 1915 to accommodate the postmen (five in 1925) and the telephone exchange (54 subscribers in 1925). The telephone exchange moved to the Maldon Road in 1929 and in September 1931, Mrs. Langman retired as sub-postmistress and was presented with a gift by 74 subscribers. The Post Office moved to 'Meadowside' (67 Main Road).

High Street, Danbury. No. 1033

11. High Street, Danbury, c1930. The motor age proper altered the whole character of the main road through Danbury. The highway was given granite kerbs and a tarmac surface about 1929. Many new buildings appeared that were geared to the increased mobility of people who could now afford a motor car. The garage, right, the second to appear along the main road, there was already one near the Bell, was built and operated by A. & H. Digby about 1925 and then taken over by Albert Hobbs about 1927. Beyond the garage is the Dainties Café which was built and opened by the Misses Curtis about 1925 to cater for the many tourists that were coming to the village. There is also a large notice in the garden of Box Cottage, left, advertising the Spinney Café, situated a little further along the road, which had been opened about 1928. Box Cottage was pulled down for road widening in 1936. The group of cottages beyond the Dainties Café, right, were all owned by the Riffhams Estate and were sold in 1918.

12. Rectory Farm, Danbury, c1915. This house is on an ancient site documented as early as 1176. In 1607 the Reverend Thomas Jennings, Rector of Willingale Spain, left it to his widow, for life, with reversion to Christ's College, Cambridge, as part of a benefaction for four poor scholars. Between 1654 and 1684 it was the Star public house. It was later christened the Star and Garter and flourished till 1805. After its demise as a public house it became a farm and in 1858 Christ's College sold the property to the Lord of the Manor who let it to the Rector. It was at about this time that the house was given the distinctive neo Tudor windows which are so characteristic of property in the village once owned by the Lord of the Manor. Mr. Albert Baker, son of the Eves Corner builder, was a tenant farmer here from about 1910 to 1920. Mr. Baker, who had six sons, is seen on his milk float. By about 1930 Mr. D.B. Tugwell had a preparatory school here.

13. The Street, Danbury, c1890. On the right is Millington House the eastern part of which dates from about 1500 but the five bay brick front of 1719 was probably built by Francis Millington who was churchwarden in 1722. In the nineteenth century this house was a 'ladies boarding academy' operated by the Ellis family; then in the 1840s it became a gentlemen's boarding academy that was run by Reverend Thomas Morrell who later became Congregational Minister at Little Baddow from 1852 to 1872. Next it became a beer and wine shop, called the Rose & Crown, kept by Frederick Cooper. After about 1875 it reverted to a private house, but was still occupied by the Coopers. John and his wife were living here in 1881 and they kept one servant. In this century Doctor P.T. Spencer Phillips of Great Baddow had a daily surgery at this house between about 1922 and 1929. The cottage, extreme left, was in 1840 a Wesleyan Chapel and its minister was Reverend Morrell who lived opposite. For Appletree Cottage, mid left, see fig. 14.

14. The Street, Danbury, c1912. This view looking west shows right, the two semi-detached Edwardian villas built about 1904 on the site of the old Pound and the other detached house Hawarden, built at the same time, but incorporating the old 1840s chapel as its rear wing. These houses were much more urban in spirit than the cottages built in the village hitherto. The first villa, Meadowside, was a school kept by Miss Hunsdon and later, for nearly twenty years it was the Post Office until its move up the hill to its present site in 1947. The second house, Danbury Villa, was the home of William Spokes, a Danbury-Chelmsford carrier, from about 1907 to 1917. His cart stands outside the gates. William Spokes was also a local bellringer and later verger at the church. Appletree Cottage, of eighteenth century date, that can be seen partly hidden by the tree, right, was a sweet shop kept by Mrs. Hannah Wakefield from 1899 till the Second World War. The brick building, left, the original brewhouse of the 'Rose & Crown', was a hairdresser's shop by 1930.

15. Griffin Hill, Danbury, c1890. This photograph shows well how erosion has entrenched the roadway which could follow the course of a Roman track. On the extreme left can be seen the shelter and pound where animals on their journey from Maldon spent the night before being driven to Chelmsford Market. At the top of the hill are the Griffin Inn and Mr. Charles Stannard's drapery and grocery store. On the extreme right can be seen the outbuildings of Millington House and on the High Path, right, a row of cottages, later refurbished by William Baker, the builder from Eves Corner. At the far end of the row in 1881 lived Joseph Campion, bootmaker, his wife and three sons one of whom was also a bootmaker and another a bootmaker's apprentice. Above the row is 'Lingwood House', formerly called 'Tankards'. A Mrs. Liddiard was there from about 1898 to 1917. The bearded man is Mr. Albert Hoar, who from about 1885 carried on the business of carpenter and undertaker at premises opposite the Griffin.

16. The Griffin, Danbury, c1908. This inn dates from about 1500 and was originally a farm house called Peppers and had 13 acres of land attached to it in 1637. The first record of this house as an inn was in 1744 when the local bellringers quaffed ale here at the expense of the Landisdale Charity. It had several distinguished guests from the 1820s onwards including Lord St. Albans, Grand Falconer of England; Sir Walter Scott; and the eccentric Father Ignatius, the self-appointed Abbot of Llanthony in Wales. In the late nineteenth century it was the meeting place of the North East London Cycle Club. In 1905 the Great Eastern Railway commenced operating a 'bus service from Chelmsford to Danbury. These steam 'buses, as shown, terminated their journey at the Griffin. The proprietor, Emil Rudin, in 1914 advertised: 'excellent family & residential accommodation; nine bedrooms & hotel lounge; tea terrace with splendid country views; motor garage & pit & good stabling.' Down the hill on the right can be seen the Edwardian villas built about 1904.

17. The Street, Danbury, c1910. On the right is one of the old steam 'buses, with its crew standing by, waiting to go to Chelmsford. Hill Cottage, left, is where David Finch, Danbury-Chelmsford carrier, lived from 1885 to 1907. Adjoining this cottage is the 'Plumber's Shop' occupied in 1881 by Ebenezer Furlong, plumber, glazier and painter. These premises were taken over by Albert Hoar about 1885 and he carried on the business of carpenter and undertaker until about 1912. It continued to be used as a plumber's shop by Sydney Willett who was replaced by the Chelmsford Star Cooperative Society. Beyond the shop is Lingwood House which was occupied in 1922 by John Herbert Beaumont. The bowler hatted character in front of Hill Cottage is Bob Barker who lived in a cottage adjoining the Cricketers. 'Old Bob' was *the forerunner of today's travelling shop, an itinerant salesman of anything he could carry. His great round basket contained nearly everything from Kippers to Bullseyes and it must have weighed a hundredweight. He always wore a bowler hat as he said it was the sign of a tradesman* (Dick Roast).

18. Danbury Rectory, c1910. This was built about 1720 on the site of an earlier Rectory. Originally this comprised a square two storey building, but in 1810 the Rector, Brook Henry Bridges, who had seven children, added the top storey shown and the south wing, left, to accommodate his increasing household. He died in 1855, aged 86. He was succeeded by his second son, Sir Thomas Pym Bridges, and during his incumbency the major restoration of the church took place in 1866-1867. He died in 1895, aged 90, to be replaced by his cousin, John Bridges Plumtre. The Reverend J.B. Plumtre MA (standing outside his front door) was a well-loved Rector. He was a modest yet rounded character in every respect. He held office in over twenty parish organisations, including the first Parish Council in 1894; Captain of the Danbury Cricket Club, heading the batting averages of 1906; bandmaster of the Danbury String Band; and chairman of the Village Club. He died, aged 68, in 1930. 'He was a fine example of friendly, happy Christianity; he enjoyed a good joke and was author of many.'

19. The Chantry, Danbury, c1915. This house dates from about 1500 but the 'mock' timbering was not added until this century. This was one of three guild houses in the village that was left by the D'Arcy family in the sixteenth century; the rent derived from these houses probably went towards paying a chantry priest to say masses for the souls of this family. In 1840 it was owned by J.R. Spencer Phillips of New Riffhams and was occupied by Widow Mason. Robert Flory, saddler and harness maker, son of Isaac who once kept the Post Office opposite, was here from about 1859 to 1887. He was followed by Charles Downing, who was practising as a saddler and harness maker until about 1935 and whose wares are displayed outside his shop. Like his predecessor Charles Downing repaired the church bell ropes, but he ceased doing this job in 1907. He was the last saddler and harness maker in the village. Charles Downing was interested in local affairs and was a Parish Councillor for nine years between 1910 and 1924.

DANBURY. 1725.

Fred Spalding.
Photo.
Chelmsford
Copyright

20. The Stores, Danbury, c1906. About 1811 the Stores, right, was the Post Office run by the Rumseys. Their daughter, **Martha**, married Isaac Flory, collar maker, in 1813. Isaac and Martha took over the Post Office but by the 1840s they were also selling barley, peas and trusses of straw and Isaac was repairing the church coffin and bell ropes. Isaac died in 1854 and the business was continued by Martha and her son John, until 1858. The Post Office was then taken over by Frederick Lee and by the 1870s the Post Office was linked with the all important telegraph system. About 1875 the Post Office moved down the hill. By 1881 Charles and Elizabeth Stannard were selling groceries and draperies and they had let the Griffin end of the premises to the Reverend F. Cornwall, the curate, and his family. Thomas Henry Freeman, Chairman of Danbury Cricket Club, was the next draper and grocer and his widow, Edith, had taken over the business by 1902. John Boreham came about 1905 and was operating 'Refreshment Rooms' in addition to the shop. He was replaced about 1909 by F. Luckin Smith, the Chelmsford provision merchants.

21. Frettons, Danbury, 1890. In essence we have here a timber house much altered and enlarged in brick between the sixteenth and nineteenth centuries. John Fretoun appears in records in 1388. For nearly 130 years from 1669 this house was owned by the Nicholls family. It then had several occupants until in 1880 it was purchased by John Timbrell Pierce, Barrister at Law, FRGS. Mr. and Mrs. Pierce had seven children and in 1881 there was a resident governess and a nurse to look after them. There were also two domestic servants. John Pierce became a churchwarden and was chairman of Danbury's first Parish Council in 1894 and he was later made a magistrate and a Deputy Lieutenant of Essex. He died in 1908. The house then had a succession of residents including Howson Devitt, insurance broker, who became a Parish Councillor in 1913, and Colonel Eustace Hill. In the 1920s the house was bought by Neville Dawson, and his son, Douglas Dawson, presented several of his father's fields near Eves Corner for the benefit of the village in 1948. (Photo ERO collection.)

DANBURY. 127.

22. Moor's Bridge, Danbury, 1894. This view shows that part of the main road bordered on the right by white railings. A small culverted stream from Frettons flows under the road here, hence the inference to a bridge, and the name Moor's comes from 'le Moores' which in 1560 was a field close to or on which the Scout Headquarters now stands. The four wheeled dog cart is carrying the Hitchcock brothers, then young boys, of Bay Lodge. The driver is Henry Mothersele, who was in the service of the Hitchcock family for 53 years. Henry Mothersele was a remarkable man. He had had very little education, but he knew the works of Shakespeare and the Bible almost by heart. He had a great interest in classical music and was a teacher at the Church Sunday School. To the right can be seen the grocery and drapery store and between that and the church the roof of the Rectory. This road was not kerbed and metalled till about 1929.

23. Main Road, Danbury, c1905. This shows the Maldon Road looking east with Frettons' fields on the right. In the background is Danbury School built in two sections on Bushey Field which was part of the Glebe. The thatched section, beyond the building shown (see fig. 24), was built in 1835 for infants and boys by the Reverend Brook Henry Bridges on land provided by Sir Brook Bridges, Lord of the Manor. So that girls could also receive some education Sir Brook Bridges, built at his own expense in 1840, the brick and slate section shown here. The principal entrance to the school was at the west end where there was originally a porch. At the turn of the century the school had about 100 pupils and the headmaster was Mr. John Fitzwater who was also church organist. He retired in 1901 and was succeeded by Mr. Ebenezer Webster who remained until 1924. He was followed by Mr. Lawrence Richards who left in 1929 to go to Godalming. During Mr. Richard's headmastership a new west classroom was added at a cost of £697 in 1927.

24. Royce's Garage, Danbury, c1930. The site of Mr. Royce's garage near the Bell, where he set up as a cycle engineer about 1912 and later as a motor engineer, was becoming somewhat cramped and not at all adequate for the motor age, so in 1926 and 1928 he bought respectively 50 foot frontage sites adjoining Danbury School and set up business as a motor engineer about 1929 where he remained until 1945. Mr. Royce is shown sitting at the wheel of the Morris Cowley, with his daughter on the wing of the car, and three of the mechanics employed at the garage. Note the Shell and BP pumps with their long hoses so that the pavement could be straddled. Behind the garage is the original section of Danbury School built in 1835. The right half of the thatched building was the school room and the left half was where the various headmasters lived. Mr. Ebenezer Webster was the last to reside there and he retired in 1924. To the extreme left can be seen the brick and slate school building of 1840.

25. Old Workhouse, Danbury, 1890. This house lies opposite the Dawson Field. It is of fourteenth century date and was originally an open hall with two cross wings. It appears to have been one of the chantries left by the D'Arcy family. In 1771 Thomas Ffytche gave it for the use of the Parish Workhouse and it remained as such until 1832 when it was divided into two tenements. Sometime during the second half of the last century the front was given a face lift and the tile hanging, a Surrey and Sussex fashion, was applied. This was probably carried out at the behest of the landlords, the Spencer Phillips, who were then living in Surrey. In 1881 the Old Workhouse was occupied by two tenants, Thomas Townsend, a jobbing gardener, and Agnes Robinson. When Baker & Sons bought the property from John Spencer Phillips in 1918 the two tenants, Mrs. Royce and Mrs. Nicholl, were paying a total annual rental of £17:16s. The characters shown second and third respectively from the left are Mrs. Nicholl and her daughter Gladys Nicholl. (Photo ERO collection.)

26. Eves Corner, Danbury. This photograph of 1890 shows William and Mary Baker, left and centre, and probably one of their daughters outside the Eves Corner premises. In 1878 William Baker of Chelmsford leased land on which stood '...a cottage Smith's Wheelwright and Painters Shop Yard and outbuildings... known as Eves Corner' shown here. He first undertook smith's and millwright's work (he repaired Danbury windmill) and then commenced building houses in 1880. He also undertook maintenance work on all the large houses in the area. By 1904 he had built 25 houses in the village with bricks from his own brickfields on Danbury Common and William had retired and his sons, Charles and Frank, had taken over the business at Eves Corner. In the early 1920s they had a new office, garage and cement store on the old site, right, and by 1926 Baker & Sons was a highly integrated concern, employing fifty men, and describing itself as 'builders, contracters, brick makers and land agents'. Not only were they repairing and building houses, but after 1922 had become specialists in restoring Essex's mediaeval churches. (Photo ERO collection.)

9506. The Pond, Danbury

27. Eves Corner Pond, Danbury, c1920. This pond was used for watering animals, but the original depression may have been formed when brick earth was dug from this area for nearby kilns in the middle ages. The cottage, right, was occupied in 1881 by John White, gardener; his wife Abigail, dressmaker; and lodger, Thomas Mead, brickmaker. Mrs. Coppin was living there in 1918 to be followed by Mr. and Mrs. Rothwell. Willow Cottage, centre, was the home in 1881 of Robert Card, blacksmith, his wife Eliza and their five children. Immediately to the left of Willow Cottage can be seen the roofs of Butts Farm. John Simmons bought it in 1842 and in 1881 his son, Thomas, was farming its 80 acres and carrying on a corn factor's business with three men and one boy. The Simmons continued to farm till 1931 when their lands were sold. However, John Hale Simmons (1866-1945) continued to reside here till 1945. He was a popular character; he was parish overseer, bellringer, an excellent cricketer and vice-captain of the Danbury XI. He was also a weekly Danbury-London carrier.

DANBURY

28. Eves Corner, Danbury, c1895. The seventeenth century house, extreme right, became Ernest Baker's cycle repair shop about 1914. It later sold confectionary under F. Lancaster and Dan Hawkins. The second house, two tenements, is of eighteenth century date and the third house, Eves Cottage, of seventeenth century date, is where Reverend Hay, Curate, in 1885 founded a reading room. This men's club sold non-alcoholic refreshments. The subscription was one penny a week and disorderly members were expelled. To the extreme left are the cottages built about 1750 on 'Hutts'. The far end of the row was a blacksmiths from about 1770 to 1879. Bob Mead (1825-1919) was living in the middle cottage in 1881 together with his wife and seven children. He was first a boot and shoemaker, then a bricklayer and in 1884 church clerk and sexton. In 1915 he retired from this last post when he was 90 years old. To the right of the row the 'Penthouse', alias Holly Cottage, marked by two chimneys, is where Willie Burr and his descendants lived from the 1840s to 1922.

29. The Baker's Arms, Danbury, c1905. Edward Hollingsworth (1771-1837), grocer, owned the shop, right, and the bakery opposite by the 1820s. His two sons Henry (1799-1847) and William (1803-1875) carried on businesses as grocer and baker respectively at the shop and the bakery. Henry, the grocer, died in 1847 and the shop was looked after by Miss Cockett, but after her death the grocer's shop was taken over by William who lived opposite. He refurbished the shop and cottages in 1871. William died in 1875 and one of his twelve children, Mrs. Fanny Webb (1850-1930), was the next grocer. Fanny married William Applebee (1855-1937), a carpenter, and first clerk to the Parish Council from 1894 to 1927. After Fanny's death the business was carried on by her son, William, who sold the shop about 1937, thus for ever severing the Hollingsworth connection. Meanwhile, beer and bread were being retailed at the bakery in the 1840s and in 1881 this was being continued by Edward Hollingsworth. Bread making had ceased before Walter Gray bought the house in 1892 and named it The Baker's Arms.

30. Belvedere Farm, Danbury, Christmas 1914. This photograph was taken by a member of the Fourth Gloucester Regiment's Inter Communications Section which had its base here and the soldiers occupied the barns and sheds during their stay in Danbury. Here some of the soldiers are photographed together with Mrs. and Mr. Rumble, the new tenants, who are shown second and fourth respectively from the left. Belvedere Farm, formerly Belvedere Place, was operative as a 42 acre farm and its fields unhindered by housing stretched into Hopping Jacks and along the Maldon Road as far as Belvedere Road. The front part of the house is probably late eighteenth century and was built by the Mason family and four generations of them resided here until taken over about 1900 by Arthur Devreux Bird and he in turn was followed by Mr. and Mrs. Rumble in 1914 and Kemp Forrester in 1916. This property was part of the Riffhams' Estate and was sold in 1918. It had farm accommodation for two horses, pigs, chickens and 13 cows. Dr. J.P. Wells was living here in 1929.

31. Hill House, Danbury, 1915. This house, left of seventeenth and eighteenth century date was the Blue Boar Inn in the early 1700s. At the beginning of the nineteenth century it was owned by John Wiggins, a wealthy property agent, who let it in 1837 to the Reverend T.P. Bridges, Curate, who vacated it when he became Rector in 1859. By 1870 it was owned and occupied by William Butler who had let it to Major Thomas Walford and then to Mrs. Sarah Howard, who was living here with her daughter in 1881 and employing a cook, housemaid, and groom. Edgar Gale Butler, 'gentleman', was here in 1886 and he was a member of Danbury's first Parish Council elected in 1894. He was followed at the house by Charles Pickersgill Smith and in 1908 by General F.F. Johnson who had fought in the Egyptian and Boer Wars. He was chairman of the Parish Council (1910-1920); a founder of the Village Hall; a member of the church choir and Choral Society. He moved to Eves Cottage about 1924 and in 1925 it became the residence of H. Remington Wilson.

32. Copt Hill, Danbury, c1900. Copt Hill is recorded in 1683 and for more than 200 years from the 1740s it was occupied by the Wackrill family. The first recorded member of this family was Robert whose son, Uriah I, had the present house built by Samuel Mascall for £18 in 1768. The Wackrills were gardeners and Uriah II (1772-1844) and James (1780-1859) advertised themselves as 'nursery and seedsmen'. James II (1807-1887) was the next occupant to be followed by James III (1838-1905) who courted and married in 1864 Frances Anne Tovell, Danbury School's first certificated teacher. James and his wife went to South Africa where James fought in the Zulu Wars. Their son William Robert was born there in 1879 and the family returned to England in 1880. William Robert (1879-1964) returned to Copt Hill in 1903 and brought his wife, Eva, with him. She held office in 17 village organisations and William who lived at Copt Hill till about 1946 was a member of the Danbury XI; bellringer for 40 years; sidesman for 59 years; and churchwarden in 1922.

33. The Chricketers, Danbury Common, c1910. William Jaggs was brewing beer here in 1832 and by 1845 he was farming the small fields opposite and also occupying the Old Armoury buildings. Cricket matches were being played on the Common and in 1837 John Jaggs, the next brewer at this house, was a member of the Danbury XI. He took over from William about 1858 when the house naturally took on the name, Cricketers' Inn, since Danbury matches were being played on the Common's Camp Ground and were to be so from about 1850 to 1900. John Jaggs was at this house until about 1880; he was the last of the farmer landlords. Change of tenant was frequent from 1880 to 1930, but George Finch was there from about 1897 to 1915. In 1882 the Cricketers contained among many other rooms: a large club room, bar, bar parlour, tap room, small cellar and small wine cellar; the outbuildings comprised: bowling shed, large workshop, thatched beer cellar, harness house and stabling. In 1901 there were two cottages, left, in the occupation of Collis and Bob Barker.

Published by Collins & Son, Chelmsford   59108·

Danbury Common

34. The Bakery, Danbury Common, c1905. This building occupies the site of what was probably Thomas Fryer's cottage in 1718. It was subsequently occupied by Mr. Ironmonger in 1767 and Charles Milward in 1794. By 1840 William Hilton farmer, miller and brickmaker of Danbury, owned the property and his tenant was William Joyce, a baker. In 1872 Mr. and Mrs. Dunmow came to this property and not only took over the bakery business, but added to it that of grocer and Danbury-Chelmsford carrier. This quaint couple from Dunmow were very religious. They found Danbury spiritually 'a dark place indeed'. The site was bought in 1886 by John Timbrell Pierce Esquire, of Frettons, barrister at law and church warden. It may have been at this time that the house was altered or reconstructed into the form shown here and it certainly looked like this in 1890. The Dunmows moved to the Runsell Bakery about 1893. There have been several occupants at the Bakery this century, including: Henry Charge, Silas Brazier, Charles Goody, John Warder and Harry Digby who last baked bread in 1959.

Woodham Road, Danbury Common

59170   Published by Collins & Son, Chelmsford

35. Woodham Road, Danbury Common, c1905. The well-proportioned house, 'Furzelea', shown right, was built by and for William Baker, the builder from Eves Corner, in 1894; and the next house, formerly 'The Glen', was built in 1904 and in 1910 Frederick Sayer was living there. William Baker came to Eves Corner in 1878 and developed a prosperous building business. Afer moving to 'Furzelea' he kept cows on the Common during the summer months. Annually in June or July nearly all his workmen were employed in haymaking in his fields adjoining the Common. His pastoral pursuits were important as he had eight children to feed and he needed hay for his horses, which were his only means of transport. William Baker was a member of the Plymouth Brethren sect and had a mission built on a site adjoining the Common. William Baker lived at 'Furzelea' until his death in 1929.

63642. DANBURY.

36. Danbury Common, c1910. William Baker, the builder of Eves Corner, had bought up a great deal of property adjoining Danbury Common. Kiln Cottages, so named because they are on or close to an eighteenth century brick kiln, shown right, were bought by William Baker in 1894. In the 1920s Fern's Hollow at this end of the row was occupied by W.F. Munnion who had a motor body building shop at the Mill. Heathcote, shown left, was built for Frank Baker of Baker & Sons in 1903. Several of the twenty or so houses, such as Heathcote, that Bakers built around the common before 1920, are of assured proportions and well-designed. Mr. Pertwee of Chelmsford may have been the architect. These building operations gave rise to the following comment in 1925: *Until quite lately when the building of rather glaringly new cottages has disturbed the mellow tones of the upland landscape, Danbury Common... was a place of entirely unspoiled beauty, but in spite of the building enterprise of recent years it retains a very pleasant atmosphere.* (Gordon Home: 'Through East Anglia'.)

On Danbury Common   59169   Published by Collins & Son, Chelmsford

37. Danbury common, c1905. The pond in the foreground obtained its water supply from the Boarded Well close to the tree, centre. The cottages, left, occupy the site of John Horne's house. He was a tiler and brickmaker in 1368 and gave his name, Horne Row, to this Common. The centre house of the three, right, used to be the Black Boy beer house. It has cellars which are said to have been used for storing illicit goods when the Common was used by the smugglers for hiding and distributing contraband. The beer house was kept by Thomas Ewers from about 1888 to 1910 when it was closed. For centuries this common had formed the grazing lands for the sheep and cattle of the St. Clere's and Herons and adjoining Manors. In 1896 it was written that: *Excursions and holidaymakers pour out of Chelmsford, Maldon and Southend to spend their days on these wide commons. There is… Horne Row with its yellow sandpits and broken ridges, its tumbled roofs and twisted chimneys half hidden among the gorse and blackberry bushes…*

38. Ludgores, Danbury Common, c1910. Great Ludgores was here in 1560 when it was occupied by Lacharge Fuller. In date the present house is probably mid-seventeenth century and refronted in the eighteenth. Although Ludgores farmhouse was in the manor of St. Clere's and Herons, Danbury, its lands stretched into the adjoining Manor of Gibcracks which until 1888 formed part of Purleigh. For over 200 years this farm was owned by the Cooper family, but by 1881 it was occupied by a Cornishman, William Henry Langman, who farmed 132 acres and employed one man and one boy. It was later occupied by William Wood and Raymond Manby. From about 1920 to 1937 it was the Reverend E.G. Falconer's Home for Motherless Children. The line of poplars marks the boundary between the farm and the common. In 1840 the land by the right hand tree was known as the 'Great Orchard'.

39. Bay Lodge, Mill Lane, Danbury, c1890. It is said that this is the site of the original mill house which was acquired by William Hilton, miller, farmer and brickmaker, in the early nineteenth century. About 1840 he rebuilt the original house and renamed it Bay Lodge. The house shown, wears its 1840s livery with gothic porch, cusped and pinnacled barge boards and ornamental chimneys. Hilton must have lived in some style for when he died in 1856 he left £80,000 and property in Danbury to his daughter, Sarah, who continued to live here until about 1882. In 1881 Miss Sarah Hilton lived here with a cook and housemaid. By 1882 Miss Emma Hitchcock was residing at Bay Lodge. In 1902 the Hitchcock family presented a memorial gate to Danbury churchyard inscribed: 'Jesus saith I am the way.' Miss Hitch-cock, who owned Well View in Copt Hill used that building as a chapel of the Plymouth Brethren from about 1894 to 1928. Miss Hitchcock was at Bay Lodge till about 1928 to be replaced by her nephew, Major F.B. Hitchcock.

40. Danbury Windmill, c1890. John Ingold of Woodham Walter was granted two acres of ground, formerly waste, in 1732. He surrendered the site in 1734 and a windmill, 'then lately erected', was on this site. The mill shown here is the one erected by Ingold, but by 1811 it had come into the hands of William Hilton who accumulated vast wealth during the Napoleonic Wars. A second windmill, probably brought from Little Baddow, was put up on this site, but this second mill had disappeared by 1858. In 1878 the mill shown was struck by lightning. *The electric fluid struck the lower sail and entered the bottom floor of the mill, wind gear and stairs and scattered them in all directions.* William Baker, of Eves Corner, a millwright by profession, repaired the mill several times, but eventually the mill was taken down before 1897 and Walter Nicholls, miller, was using a steam mill (now Bow Scaffolding). In the background is 'Mill House' of eighteenth century date which was occupied by George White, miller, in 1881.

41. Runsell Green, Danbury, c1905. Here houses cluster around a roughly triangular green. This hamlet formed the nucleus of a separate Manor called Runsell which was given to Canterbury Cathedral by Brithnoth before the Battle of Maldon in 991. The brick house, left, was originally the Anchor kept by the Wiggins family, but about 1830 lost its sign to the house across the road. By the end of the 1830s the original Anchor now carried the sign of the Saracen's Head which had at least thirteen landlords before it was closed about 1908. Harvest Home suppers were held there in the nineteenth century. The Saracen's Head continued as a bakery and grocery shop well into this century. Meanwhile, the Anchor across the road was brewing and retailing beer. Its landlords were members of the Wiggins family who were there from about 1855 to 1905. The bakery, mid left, was being operated by Cyril and Stanley Upson (see fig. 42). Gill House, right, of fifteenth century date, was occupied from about 1865 to 1900 by George Ager, described first as a pig killer and later as a pork butcher.

42. The Bakery, Runsell Green, Danbury, c1905. James Bunn was the first recorded baker and grocer here in the 1880s. At the 1881 census James had six children four of whom were old enough to attend school. James Bunn was baking till the early 1890s and he was replaced by William Dunmow who added the function of Danbury-Chelmsford carrier to his baking and grocery business. He was also a local preacher and he ran a Sunday School here for thirty children in connection with the Gay Bowers Mission. He was replaced about 1900 by Henry Hicks and by 1905 the new owners were Cyril and Stanley Upson who employed James Bunn, now nearly ninety years, holding the horse, left. Mrs. Upson is standing in the doorway of the shop and Teddy Kemp, another employee, is seen to the right holding another horse. In 1915 this business was bought by Mr. E.A. Roast who had four horses and carts to cover his rounds before buying a model T Ford in 1925 which reduced his reliance on horses. The Bakery closed in 1961.

43. Cherry Garden Lane, Danbury, c1910. This lane, looking west, is so called because Mr. Crussell had cherry orchards backing on to it. The two late eighteenth century thatched cottages right belonged to the Speakman family and were inhabited by Mr. and Mrs. Willie Medley and Peter Smith who was a coalman. Holly Cottage, centre, of eighteenth century date and burned down in the 1950s, was occupied by Mr. and Mrs. Purkiss and their large family. In the background can be seen 'Brockham' built by Henry Godfrey about 1909. Mr. Godfrey, of H. and T.C. Godfrey of Chelmsford, had previously lived at 'Wildcroft' on Danbury Common. While at Brockham the Godfreys owned the land on which Somerley, Lawlings and Hyde Green are built as well as fields behind the house on which there were buildings. This small farm supplied milk to local residents. Mr. Bill Fitch helped to run the farm and look after the garden. Mrs. Godfrey and her daughters, Grace and May, were keen on the Band of Hope and annually held tea and games on the site of Somerley.

"GAY BOWERS." DANBURY, ESSEX.

44. Gay Bowers House, Danbury, c1912. This was owned by the Trussell family in 1840 and they were still there in 1881 when Sarah Trussell, then 84, and her nephew George were farming the 84 acres with five men and one boy. The Trussells were followed by the Byfords who had previously owned the paper Mills at Little Baddow. About 1904 Edwin Kerwin, JP, came to reside here and his two sons, Clifford and Charles, were involved in the Coronation celebrations for George V in 1911. The Kerwins farmed here until about 1920. During the First World War this was one of the many properties in the area where soldiers were billeted before going to France. The correspondence on this card, postmarked 20 August 1914, says: 'We arrived here about 9 o'clock last night, 20 miles from Brentwood [they had obviously marched]. We slept in barns belonging to this house. Of course, we had clean straw to lie on. We see life, don't we? We are having this day off and moving on tomorrow.' The Kerwins were replaced by George Starkey and then by John Slight about 1925.

45. Gay Bowers Manor, Danbury, c1908. In 1895 this was described as 'the large, low, many windowed house... which figures prominently in Joseph Strutt's 'Queenhoo Hall', to which Sir Walter Scott wrote the concluding chapter'. The house is clearly older as it was owned by Owen de Pier, cook, who died in 1614. The Ray family owned the house from about 1700 to 1825 when it was left to Charles Downes, gentleman, of Chelsea. By 1882 the house was owned by the Reverend John Compton who appears to have rejected the views of the Church of England and was holding services on Runsell Green. In 1883 he erected a corrugated iron mission, seating 300, in the grounds of the house, but by 1887 he had left and the mission was sold. Between 1887 and 1921 the Manor had two owners, Henry Walpole George Dashwood and Edgar Price, before being bought by Sir Sydney Rowlatt (1862-1945) a judge of the High Court, King's Bench Division. In 1930 he was Assize Judge at Chelmsford.

46. Cottage in the Bush, Little Baddow, c1900. This cottage overlooks Patten Well and Danbury village. In 1620 'Humfrey Hedge held a messuage with garden containing ½acre... lying on the Comon next Danbury which was lately old Hartes', for which he paid 6d and two hens yearly. It is mentioned in 1696 as 'the house in the Bush' being 'the mansion house' of Daniel Cornewell. In turn Cornewell conveyed it to John Burchell in 1710 and four generations of this family were tenants (SVR). In 1881 Simon Balls, an agricultural labourer, and Sarah, his wife, were here. About 1900 the cottage was let to Mr. Wackrill, a Danbury nurseryman, and he is seen here together with his wife looking over the hedge. Later, in 1945, the cottage was bought by Dr. C. Armstrong Gibbs (1889-1960), the Essex composer. He had the cottage enlarged and lived here till 1960. Armstrong Gibbs is most famous for his catchey song, 'Dusk', adapted from his 'Fancy Dress Suite', and some of Walter de la Mare's works which he set to music.

47. Pattentees, The Ridge, Little Baddow, c1930. This name is partly derived from Patten Well that existed on the other side of the road on Lingwood Common. This eighteenth century house was originally called Hammonds, but was given the present name in the early nineteenth century. By the 1830s it was owned by Thomas Docwra who paid £210 for the house, barn, cowhouse, outbuildings, yard, garden in front and rear and an acre of pasture adjoining (SVR). In 1839 William Docwra, a Quaker, who also owned Garland's Farm, Runsell Green, was the owner and it was let to Samuel Ratcliff. In 1881 it was occupied by Thomas Enefer, a woodman, Alice, his wife, a dressmaker, and their nine-month-old-daughter, Edith. The bungalow next to Pattentees, left, is on the site of previous cottages and the next three dwellings, all twentieth century, occupy a croft that was known as Winlesses in 1677. About 1924 Dr. C. Armstrong Gibbs, the Essex composer, had built himself a new house, Crossings, opposite these bungalows.

48. Woodlands, Little Baddow, 1891. This house could have been built by Mr. Meggy, proprietor of the Chelmsford Chronicle, about 1800. He was living there in 1840. By the 1870s it was occupied by Benjamin Livermore whose father once operated the Paper Mills. In 1882 Miss Clarissa Livermore gave a penny and a hot cross bun to each pupil of the National School on Good Friday, but this celebration was postponed until Easter Monday in case it led to undue levity on such a holy day! (SVR). When this photograph was taken Mrs. Ady, widow of the Archdeacon, was living here. Early this century Mr. Phillip Boldero, a retired but prosperous draper, bought Woodlands. The Bolderos were most generous to the Parish. Miss Boldero was found in 1915 addressing the school children 'on their position and work in the state'. After Mr. Boldero's death in 1919 his widow moved to 'Scapa' and in 1925 she gave a new bell to St. Mary's in memory of her husband. The occupant in the 1920s was Major Hugh Luard, a descendant of a prominent Essex family. (Photo ERO collection.)

49. Thatched Cottage, Little Baddow, c1910. The cottage was part of the New Riffhams' Estate and had been built by 1830 on land called 'The Gapp' (SVR). The road in the foreground was a private way to Riffhams and that is why it was gated, right. The road was closed for one day a year to indicate that it was a private and not public right of way. The cottage was called Upper Lodge in the 1881 census when William and Elizabeth Dace were living there. William was an agricultural labourer and so was his second son, aged 16, but his elder son, aged 20, was a pensioner! It was called 'Fern Cottage' in the 1890s. Several families have lived there in this century including: Mr. and Mrs. Bains; Mr. and Mrs. Wallace Binder, Wallace was later Mayor of Maldon; Mr. and Mrs. Guy Puddephatt; and by 1924 it had been bought by Ernest Arnold of J.H. Clarke & Company of Chelmsford, who renamed it 'The Thatched Cottage'. (Photo PC.)

1872   Old Riffans, Little Baddow

Fred Spalding
Photo
Chelmsford
Copyright

50. Old Riffhams, Little Baddow, c1910. This probably occupies the site of a house associated with the mediaeval Manor of Riffhams. This present house, originally of timber construction, dates from the sixteenth century, but was enlarged in brick in the eighteenth century. In the early nineteenth century the property was owned by J.R. Spencer Phillips Esquire, who built himself a 'new lodge' in Danbury. However, Old Riffhams remained part of his estate and from about 1890 it was occupied by Charles Smoothy, the estate gamekeeper. He was a keen ornithologist and taxidermist and his fine collection of birds is now in the Chelmsford Museum. By about 1912 Reverend George Woolley and his family were here. One son, Sir Leonard, an archaeologist, directed important excavations at Ur between 1922 and 1934. Another son, the Reverend Geoffrey, was awarded the first ever Territorial Officer Victoria Cross in 1915. In 1919 the house was bought by Mr. Herbert Paterson, a loyal Congregationalist, who has left us with many interesting black and white sketches of the Danbury and Little Baddow area. He was there for more than thirty years.

51. The Dairy, Riffhams, Little Baddow, c1910. Although in Little Baddow this house was part of the New Riffhams' Estate, Danbury, but it was only a stone's throw from the main house. The Dairy was built by J.R. Spencer Phillips before 1841, for in that year Prudence Tween, 'dairy woman', was living there with her husband, an agricultural labourer (SVR). It was called the 'Dairy Farm' in 1881 and Joseph and Elizabeth Hinton were residing there with their family. Joseph was a gardener, probably at New Riffhams, his son, George, aged 16 was a Post Office messenger and his other son, Joseph, aged 14, was a butcher. The two daughters Fanny and Alice were still at school. When this view was taken the Riffhams' gardener was Mr. Richardson. He is seen here with his wife, his son Albert and his daughter Muriel. Much later The Dairy became known as the White House.

52. Little Graces, Little Baddow, 1891. Sir Henry Mildmay in his will of 1637 mentions 'ould Dales' purchased from John and Robert Haward. This seventeenth century house may originally have been called 'Dales' and was so named after 'Dales Green' which was higher up the road near New Riffhams. In 1811 Mr. Fletcher was living at Little Graces with his servant, John Burchell (SVR). By 1840 it was owned by Sir Brook William Bridges and tenanted by John Simmons, a member of the well-known farming family of Danbury and Little Baddow. Later in the nineteenth century Little Graces was divided into two cottages and in 1881 it was occupied by two agricultural labourers: James Mason and Samuel Oliver. The son of the latter was a grocer's assistant, aged 14. This house remained as two separate tenements until well into this century and when the late George Saunders of Runsell Green lived here with his parents until 1910 it was known as the 'Wood Yard'. (Photo ERO collection.)

53. Great Graces, Little Baddow, 1891. It owes its name to the family of Le Gras, Lords of the Manor in the thirteenth century. The Manor passed to the D'Arcy family in the fourteenth century and Sir Thomas probably rebuilt the house in brick about 1540. Eventually Sir Henry Mildmay bought Graces and was probably responsible for the outbuildings and may have laid out Grace's Walk (SVR). It is tragic that in 1615 the pretty Lady Alice Mildmay drowned herself in a pond by reason of her husband's unkindness. Her ghost still haunts Grace's by the bridge that crosses Sandon Brook halfway down the walk. The house of about 1540 was large and possessed 26 hearths in 1672, but during the first half of the nineteenth century it was partly demolished and reduced to a farm house. In 1840 the house was owned by Sir Brook William Bridges (1801-1872) and occupied by John Phelp Simmons. By 1881 it was being farmed by Joseph Yell who employed eight men and two boys. The Yells farmed here for more than half a century. (Photo ERO collection.)

LITTLE BADDOW. 382

54. Miss Sorrell's Shop, Little Baddow, c1910. Mrs. Sarah Sorrell was operating a grocery shop, right, in 1851 and in 1861 she was being assisted by her son, Stephen. By 1871 Stephen had died and his widow, Julia, had married Samuel Campion. Samuel ran the grocery and Julia the drapery side of the business. Widowed again Julia took over the Post Office from Mr. Horth about 1886 and about 1890 she was succeeded by her niece, Elizabeth Sorrell, who remained postmistress until 1930 (SVR). The shop closed in 1970. Behind the hedge, right, is Bellevue where George Aylett and later Percy Puddephatt had a butcher's shop. Beyond, behind the tree, is the old British School, closed 1895, which was leased to the Parish Council for community use. In January 1922, the old school, now enlarged and altered by Mr. D. Marven, builder and former pupil, was opened by Lady Rasch as the village's memorial to the fallen of the First World War. The Memorial Hall was burned down in April 1959. The gable of the Almshouses, centre, can be seen in the distance.

LITTLE BADDOW. 1746.

Fred Spaldin
Photo
Chelmsford
Copyrig

55. Colam Lane, Little Baddow, c1905. On the left is Ann's Cottage of late eighteenth century date. It once belonged to Jeremiah Pledger and was purchased in 1830 by the Butler School Charity and sold by them in 1907. Andanburies (Aldermanburg) Farm can just be discerned right, between the trees. Its land once stretched as far as Parsonage Lane and the General's Arms was later built on it (SVR). In 1881 James Smith, master boot maker, lived here with his wife, Edith, and nineteen year old son, Edgar, who was described as 'Worker Electric Light'. Charles Shipman, carpenter and wheelwright, was at Aldermanburg from about 1885 to the end of the First World War. Miss Beatrice Shipman, Charles' daughter, was a dairy farmer here before the 1920s and her cows grazed on the Rodney Fields. She also possessed a great variety of geese, ducks and chickens, and one of her geese used to follow her all over the village. The house and land was sold for development in 1976.

THE RECTORY, LITTLE BADDOW. 1745.

56. The Rectory, Little Baddow, c1905. Although they owned Parsonage Farm there was no official residence in the Parish for the Rectors. Therefore, when Reverend (later Archdeacon) W. Ady, MA, was appointed Rector in 1847 (he had been Curate and Vicar previously) he decided to build a new Rectory. William Butterfield (1811-1902) was appointed architect and he built the Rectory in a style that was inimitably his with much use of polychromatic brickwork. (His greatest work is All Saints' Margaret Street, London.) Archdeacon Ady was a very energetic and forceful character in the village. He was followed by the Reverend F.T. Tayler, MA, Rector from 1882 to 1915, and then by the Reverend Jesse Berridge, AKCL, (1878-1966) who was here from 1916 to 1948. The Reverend (later Canon) Berridge was a much loved Rector. He was an antiquarian of no mean distinction. He served on the Council of the Essex Archaeological Society; he helped to set up the Essex Record Office; he wrote five historical novels based on the local milieu; and contributed local history articles to the Essex Review. (Photo PC.)

LITTLE BADDOW. 571.

57. Holybreds Lane, Little Baddow, c1905. Chestnut Cottage, left, was known as Langores in the early 1400s and Cuckoos Cottage in the 1800s. The present cottage is probably eighteenth century in date. It was occupied early this century by two extraordinary sisters, Emma and Eliza Scotchman. Cuckoos, centre, a farmhouse of sixteenth century date, is famous for being the meeting place of nonconformists from about 1660. It is also traditionally the place to which Thomas Hooker came in 1629 to operate a school after losing his lectureship at St. Mary's, Chelmsford. Hooker was assisted here by another Cambridge graduate, John Eliot. Both these men enjoyed the friendship of John Newton, Rector of Little Baddow, himself 'a very uneasy conformist' (RBK) and both settled in New England and became famous there. Cuckoos had two tenants in 1881: the farmer's widow, Ann Gibling, who lived there with a servant, and farm bailiff Samuel Smith, who had five children. There have been several farmers here since 1900 including George Enefer, John Baker, William Addison and William Wilde.

58. United Reformed Church and Manse, Little Baddow, c1900. Nonconformity was greatly influenced from about 1650 by Sir Gobert Barrington, Lord of the Manor of Tofts and owner of Cuckoos, his wife, and their son Francis. In 1708 Francis Barrington conveyed Bridge Croft to Thomas Leavesley, Minister, and four others so that a meeting house, left, could be erected. It was licensed in January 1709. Lady Barrington willed and Francis gave money to the trustees. During the ministry of the Reverend William Parry a new Manse, right, was built in 1794 and it accommodated Parry's school and dormitories. After Parry left there followed the long and popular ministries of the Reverend Stephen Morrell and his son Thomas, who between them were here from 1799 to 1877. They were followed by the Reverend David Hollies who arrived in 1878 and by the Reverend J. Stanley. During the latter's ministry the galleries were removed and new pews and an organ provided. The Reverend James Burgess came in 1902 and he turned the Manse garden into a show place. In 1907, the two hundredth anniversary, £240 was raised to build a Sunday School. The Reverend Burgess was replaced by the Reverend James Learmount in 1916 (SVR and RBK).

59. The Forge, Little Baddow, c1923. This site was originally called Heards and is recorded in 1489. This eighteenth century house served as a small farm until the nineteenth century (SVR). In 1840 this property was occupied by William Gowlett and others. By 1859 John Riley, wheelwright, had set up business here and he appears to have been succeeded by William Willers, blacksmith, whose 17 year old son was following the same occupation in 1881. James Everett, however, was well-established here in the 1890s as an agricultural engineer. His children were very much involved in Parish affairs. Wilfred was an assistant overseer to be followed into that office by his sister, Emily, in 1917. Emily became the first woman Parish Clerk in 1923 and was Clerk to the Parish Council from 1925 to 1956. Meanwhile, Albert, who lived at Gunbies till 1949, assisted at the Forge and after his father's death continued the business into the late 1950s. This photograph shows from left to right: Albert Prior; Archie Everett, James' second son; and Emily Everett, who died in 1966. (Photo PC.)

60. St. Mary's Church, Little Baddow, 1891. The Saxon lords had no doubt built a church and hall, separated by a deep lane, on the existing sites. The north wall of the nave could have been built by Germund, Lord of the Manor, in the late eleventh century. About 1340 the nave was extended southwards to accommodate two wooden effigies, a man and his wife, beneath two beautiful canopied recesses. The church also displays later features: a mid-fourteenth century tower and a fifteenth century chancel (containing Sir Henry Mildmay's tomb, who died in 1639); as well as a more than life-size wall painting of St. Christopher executed about 1380, covered up with limewash in the eighteenth century and uncovered by the Reverend Jessie Berridge in 1921. He also had the bells restored in 1925. This view shows the church covered with a muddy looking plaster; the land abutting the road, left, given by Lord Rayleigh in 1855; the line of trees behind the church marking the boundary of the old churchyard before Lord Rayleigh had given land for enlarging the churchyard in 1910. (Photo ERO collection.)

61. Little Baddow Hall, 1891. This part of the parish has been designated a 'lost village'. There is no evidence as yet to prove this. The church, hall and few cottages have probably always formed an isolated hamlet here within the parish. Beneath its nineteenth century plastered livery, the Hall, occupying an older site, is of fourteenth and fifteenth century timber construction. Its predecessor served as the Manor House of the Norman manor of Beadewan and later the Hall Manor. Prominent nineteenth century occupants were James and Kate Tweed. In 1881 they were employing eight men and four boys on the farm. They had three children, a cook and a housemaid. In 1897 Jubilee celebrations were held here with sports followed by a high tea on the lawn for about 400 adults and children. The Tweeds left about 1900 and, finally, after several tenants, the Hall was bought by Mr. and Mrs. Stuart MacDonald in 1928. They made the Hall fields into apple orchards, thus adding another interesting variation to the parish landscape. (Photo ERO collection.)

62. Little Baddow Mill, c1893. In 1777 William Johnson bought this mill and 24 acres for £2,000. He later took Johnson Clark into partnership who put up the mill for sale in 1811. It then had five pairs of stones and dealt in 375 tons of coal a year at its wharf. John Piggot bought the mill for £3,600 in 1824 and operated it till 1880. In 1863 they dealt in 448 quarters of wheat, 2,927 sacks of flour and 860 tons of coal. The mill and 13 acres of land were sold in 1880 to Edward Morgan for £2,000. Gradually the milling and coal trades declined and early in 1893 this beautiful mill was burned down. The site eventually came into the hands of the Chelmer & Blackwater Navigation Company. They built a house on the site which was let, first, to George Smith, who operated a refreshment house and coal business, and then in 1911 to William King who continued the business. In the late 1920s, his widow, Mrs. Matilda King, was a shopkeeper plying teas and refreshments.

63. Little Baddow School, c1920. There was a Church of England school in the village as early as 1836 and Frederick Phillips was the head-teacher. The white brick house shown was purchased in 1846 for £300 for use as a school. In 1847 the school had become associated with the National Society which promoted education on the lines of the established church. Lord Rayleigh and Reverend Ady were managers. The house proved inadequate as a school and a new red brick building was added in 1851. It cost £122:14:2d. Mr. Benjamin Horth, a very literate and keen headteacher, had been appointed by 1850 and he also ran the Post Office from the School House. Pupils paid 1d a week from 1847 until education became free in 1891. A new Infants' Room and enlarged School Room were additions made in 1895 (SVR). Benjamin Horth resigned in 1886 and his successors were: James Porter, William Thomas, George Taylor, Frederick Barker, Mrs. Jane Barker, Mrs. Hammond and Mrs. Turner, who was there when the school closed in 1960. The man on the right is Bill 'Diver' Marsh, road-man. (Photo PC.)

LITTLE BADDOW. 378

64. North Hill, Little Baddow, c1903. The two cottages in the foreground, right, built about 1800, were occupied by John Gibson and others in 1840. In this century, the first and second cottages were occupied respectively by Mr. Ager, pigkiller, and Mr. Humphries. Lower down the hill there were two more slate roofed weather boarded cottages built about 1800 with an eighteenth century mansard roofed house adjoining. In 1840 this row was occupied by Samuel Howard who was operating the Queen's Head beer house in the oldest part by 1851 (SVR). About 1900 the oldest cottage of the three had become Mr. Dowsett's shop. Mr. Thomas Dowsett left the village just before the First World War to live in Little Totham. His relative, Miss Edith Langford, then took over the shop and was there until well into the 1940s. Meanwhile the pair of cottages adjoining the shop, going downhill, were occupied by Bill 'Diver' Marsh, roadman, and Mrs. Short. The hedgerow, left, is the garden of Thomas Peacock, born 1831, shoemaker, who is remembered for his white, near waist long hair and beard.

Baddow Rodney

65. Baddow Rodney, c1905. This view is from the bottom of York Street, the track to the left, looking towards the Old Rodney, centre. This area, later to become known as the Heather Hills, comprised some 16 acres. It once belonged to Lord Rayleigh, Lord of the Manor, then to Mr. H.J. Martin and, finally, in May 1922, it was bought, together with the Old Rodney, by Mr. and Mrs. Reginald Clark who eventually sold it, at a reasonable sum, to Mr. and Mrs. Gregory Nicholson of Dukes Orchard. In 1925 Mr. and Mrs. Gregory Nicholson kindly presented the Heather Hills to the village so that they should be open to the public for all time. 'The bramble and bracken, the steep slopes, the wide view, the heather, the seclusion, the liberty to wander that the place offers, make it favourite playground,' so wrote Reverend Jesse Berridge, local author and Rector, in 1925. Within this area lies a roughly circular, but denuded, rampart that may well be Iron Age in date.

66. The Rodney, North Hill, Little Baddow, c1930. This eighteenth century building was described as a cottage with garden in 1840. It was owned by Thomas Hodge and occupied by James Edwards. By the late 1840s Charles Smith was a baker, grocer and beer seller here, so it was only natural that he took over about 1867 the discarded Rodney sign from up the hill. Charles Smith continued with his trade as baker and even after his death his widow, Mrs. Lois Smith, continued as a baker and publican, but was assisted in 1881 by her brother, Jacob Barnard. Before 1900 her son, Herbert Smith, had taken over the bakery and beer trade which did not cease until the arrival of a new landlord, Sidney Wager, about 1905. Down to 1929 there was a succession of landlords here including George Collins, Edward Russell and Edward Bickmore. (Photo PC.)

67. Gunbies, North Hill, Little Baddow, c1925. The name of Gunby goes back to at least 1563. The site of Gunbies, now Fern Cottage, appears to have been divided into two at some stage and then, later, in the eighteenth century, the present house, was built on the two sites. This is shown in 1800 when Jeremiah Pledger was admitted to 'all those two messuages or tenements... commonly called or known by the name of Great Gunbies' (SVR). This house remained in the ownership of the Pledgers until 1915 when it was bought, freehold, by Mrs. H.S. Howe who sold it in 1923 to Mrs. L. Everett, wife of Albert Everett, employed by his father at the Forge. Mrs. Everett, seen here at the front door, was the village music teacher and one time organist at Little Baddow Church. After his wife's death Mr. Everett returned to the Forge in 1949 to live with his sister. Between 1900 and 1923 Gunbies had several tenants including Adam Eve, Mr. and Mrs. Bob Martin, a one time woodman, and Gerard Peacock. (Photo PC.)

68. Cock Farm, Little Baddow, circa 1900. This is an eighteenth century house on a very old site. Beer was brewed here as early as 1475 and before 1614 it was an alehouse. The 'Cock' was occupied in 1672 by Peter Foster and tax was paid on four hearths. The Fosters remained in occupation here until the nineteenth century (SVR). In 1840 John Foster owned and occupied the cottage which had a garden and orchard attached. The 1881 census shows Charles Rumsey, a dealer, living here with his 70-year-old-mother. This photograph shows Henry ('Podger') Davis, the occupier of Cock Farm, who was an ex-policeman and step-father to Miss Edith Langford who kept the small shop opposite the Rodney Inn. Henry Davis died in November 1907, aged 58. The next resident was Mr. Jackson. The man to the left is thought to be 'Captain' Peacock. (Photo PC.)

69. Colraines, Little Baddow, c1900. In the early eighteenth century Lord Colraine acquired two cottages on this site and built a hunting lodge called Colraine's Box. In 1777 it was described in particulars of Lord Barrington's estate, as 'a very convenient modern built Brick House, sash windows, good Garden, Coach House, Stable, etc.' and it was let to Thomas Hodges, later miller at the Paper Mills, for £10 a year. He was succeeded in 1780 by the Reverend Arthur Johnson, Vicar, and later by Thomas Dennis who kept it as a butcher's shop about 1820 (SVR). Mrs. Dennis was continuing the business in 1851. Simon Snow, previously of the Paper Mills, was farming Colraines in 1881 with nine men and three boys. He was followed in the 1890s by John Conbrough, also a farmer, and after his death about 1908, his widow, Mrs. Christina Conbrough, had apartments at Colraines. Some of her clientele were London artists and one of them painted a portrait of old Mr. Thomas Peacock, the boot and shoe maker, which was hung in the Royal Academy.

70. Paper Mills or Huskards Mill, Little Baddow, 1891. This mill was recorded in 1338. In 1792 there were two mills on this site: one making paper and another grinding wheat. Thomas Hodges operated one mill and the other had been let to John Livermore who made paper until about 1820. Benjamin Livermore operated a mill until the 1850s and he was followed by Simon Snow, farmer, who allied the coal trade with that of milling and landings of coal averaged 155 tons a year from 1863 to 1866. Frank Cantrell was there in the 1870s and in 1870 his coal and wheat trade amounted to 100 tons and 510 quarters respectively. In 1875 Pharoah Byford bought the mill and he continued the coal business averaging 72 tons a year between 1882 and 1884. He is described in the 1881 census as a miller and farmer employing five men and two boys. The mill was sold in 1898. The new owners used it for manufacturing carbons for electric searchlights. This photograph shows the last remaining mill on the site that was burned down about 1905. (Photo ERO collection.)

71. Paper Mills Bridge, Little Baddow, c1900. This bridge was so called because it was built adjacent to two mills one of which made paper. The bridge shown, demolished in 1935, was undoubtedly designed by the great canal engineer, John Rennie. At this point the Chelmer & Blackwater Navigation, opened 1797, was too wide to have a single span brick bridge, so substantial brick abutments were built either side of a heavy supporting timber structure. The barge shown is making its way to Heybridge. These horse-drawn barges were 60 feet long and 16 feet of beam and had a draught of only 2 feet. The commodities carried to Chelmsford were coal (25,000 tons a year in the 1830s), timber, lime, wheat and dung; and to Heybridge, bricks and flour. As the nineteenth century progressed so the railway had its effects upon water transport and this is demonstrated clearly by the declining amounts of coal reaching Chelmsford: in 1866: 10,724 tons; in 1890: 4,840 tons; and in 1914 only 2,456 tons.

72. Lock Cottage, Little Baddow, c1910. This cottage, now replaced, must have been built just before the opening of the Chelmer & Blackwater Navigation in 1797. Paper Mills Lock was a strategic point on the navigation as it was used as a half-way house for the barges plying between Springfield and Heybridge Basin. Prior to 1914 it was not uncommon for about eight barges to draw up outside the cottage at nightfall, so that the horses could spend the night in the nearby stables and the bargees slept in the bothy, now the Company's offices, opposite. Members of the Marven family were employed on the navigation earlier this century and two members of this family are sitting on the balance beam of the lock gate.

73. Mill Cottage, Little Baddow, c1906. A windmill operated by William Rotherham in 1702 and John Richardson in 1735 stood to the east of this seventeenth century cottage. About 1805 another mill was erected between the first mentioned mill and the cottage by Josiah Craneis who acquired this dwelling from Abraham Ager and later renamed it Mill Cottage. The 'new' mill was tenanted by William Hilton of Danbury and it was he who probably removed the mill to Danbury. In 1840 Mill Cottage belonged to the Riffhams' estate and was occupied by Charles Smith and in 1881 one of its two tenants was Charles Lucking, a well borer and sinker. Mill Cottage was sold in 1918 and was described as an: 'Old Fashioned Cottage... containing three Bedrooms, Sitting Room, Living Room, Kitchen and Pantry and outside Wash-house and E.C. Water is laid on to the Kitchen.' It was tenanted at £8 a year by William Lucking who was a huckster. Through the trees can be seen Ridgehurst, built in 1905 by Walter Warsop, where he carried on the business of cricket bat making.

74. The Old Rodney, Little Baddow, 1905. Before 1620 this was the site of Warren House. Part of the present structure is probably eighteenth century and by 1777 James Jordan was keeping it as the Cock & Warren alehouse. It was renamed the Rodney or Rodney Head in the late eighteenth century and was taken over by John Pullen and about 1820 by his widow, Mary. After the Rodney sign moved down the hill in the late 1860s (SVR), this property became known as the Old Rodney. About 1885 Elijah Mecklenburg opened up pleasure gardens here and it became a popular venue for Sunday School and choir outings. In 1896 the Wickham Bishops juvenile choir was conveyed here in three horse-drawn vehicles and in July 1898, 80 members of the Women's Liberal Association came in brakes for their summer excursion. By 1902 the new proprietor, Mr. William Boreham, was entertaining parishioners to a Coronation party. From May 1922, Mrs. Jessie Clark was operating the premises as the 'Old Rodney Hotel' advertising 'lunches, teas and hard tennis courts'. It became a private house in 1948.

75. Well Cottage, Little Baddow, c1910. Richard Saward, bricklayer, in 1817 built himself a cottage with barn stable and outbuildings on land taken from the waste adjoining Well Piece, a small field at the rear of Coldham Well. He called it Well Cottage and lived there until 1866 paying a rent of 1s. a year (SVR). Coldham Well was an important public well and originally the water for the Old Rodney was drawn here and conveyed on a donkey cart. In 1881 Well Cottage was occupied by William Denny, a coachman. It seems that he was freelance rather than employed by a household. George Ager, a carpenter and undertaker, was living here before 1900. He used a hand bier to wheel the coffins to the church (SVR). Between the trees, right, is Bellevue. The far end was occupied by James Mulley who was a Chelmsford carrier from the 1890s to about 1908. Bellevue Cottages were part of the Riffhams' Estate and were sold in 1918. The Post Office (Miss Sorrell's) is shown to the left of the road. (Photo PC.)

76. Wedlock Green, Little Baddow, c1910, looking towards Woodham Walter. This area was known as Loves Green in 1576 and as Whitlocks Green in 1810. It became Wedlock Green in the 1820s (SVR). This last name was emphasised and made more permanent in 1895 with the building of Wedlock Cottage by Mr. and Mrs. James Woodward (its garden with linen hanging out can be seen to the left of the road) on land known in 1620 as Willketts Croft. In 1905 the whole of Willketts, except for Wedlock Cottage, was sold to Mr. Lionel Came who had Elm Bank built and the land planted as an orchard. He was probably Little Baddow's first, albeit weekly, London commuter. On the right can be seen the house called 'Sunnymead' which was built before 1900 by Mr. Samuel Hopwood, a retired carver and gilder. This house was later occupied by his grandson, Mr. Francis Thorrington, a long serving Parish Councillor. Wedlock Green formed part of what was historically called Warren Common. This Green was linked to the Warren Farm area by a highway called Loves Lane which was later renamed York Street.